Woman Reading
to the Sea

THE BARNARD WOMEN POETS PRIZE

Edited by Saskia Hamilton

2003 *Figment*   Rebecca Wolff
       Chosen by Eavan Boland and Claudia Rankine

2004 *The Return Message*   Tessa Rumsey
       Chosen by Jorie Graham

2005 *Orient Point*   Julie Sheehan
       Chosen by Linda Gregg

2006 *Dance Dance Revolution*   Cathy Park Hong
       Chosen by Adrienne Rich

2007 *Woman Reading to the Sea*   Lisa Williams
       Chosen by Joyce Carol Oates

BARNARD WOMEN POETS PRIZE CITATION

by Joyce Carol Oates

Woman Reading to the Sea contains poems of arresting intelligence, precision, and beauty. In wonderfully crafted language, with the startling subtlety of certain of Emily Dickinson's poems, Lisa Williams takes us into eerily imagined worlds—the interior of a jellyfish, and the interior of a glacier; she beguiles us with the most seductive of poetic possibilities—that we might be absorbed into the consciousness of the beautiful and inarticulate world of nature, for instance—only to draw back in rebuke: "But this would be a lie." ("Grackles," p. 71). Williams's subject is the "tune without a mind"of the world beyond the human, and our yearning to enter it: "Is it a thing we build outside ourselves / that gives us so much purpose?" ("Field," p. 70).

The consolations of art, if not transcendence, are examined in a sequence of wonderfully evocative, candidly observant poems about Italian churches and their efforts of "restoration"; Williams brings to this familiar genre a freshness and modesty that are warmly engaging. This slender volume constitutes a journey of sorts, a pilgrimage "out" that returns the questing poet, imagined as a companion "you," to her own life. Lisa Williams is a poet of lyric gifts blessed with a luminous intelligence and wit.

ALSO BY LISA WILLIAMS

The Hammered Dulcimer

Woman Reading to the Sea

POEMS

Lisa Williams

W. W. NORTON & COMPANY

New York · London

For information about permission to reproduce selections from this
book, write to Permissions, W. W. Norton & Company, Inc.,
500 Fifth Avenue, New York, NY 10110

For information about special discounts for bulk purchases, please
contact W. W. Norton Special Sales at specialsales@wwnorton.com
or 800-233-4830

Manufacturing by The Courier Companies, Inc.
Book design by Charlotte Staub
Production manager: Andrew Marasia

Library of Congress Cataloging-in-Publication Data

Williams, Lisa, 1966–
    Woman reading to the sea : poems / Lisa Williams.—1st ed.
        p. cm.
    ISBN 978-0-393-06643-2
    I. Title.
    PS3573.I449754W66 2008
    811'.54—dc22   2007040487

W. W. Norton & Company, Inc.
500 Fifth Avenue, New York, N.Y. 10110
www.wwnorton.com

W. W. Norton & Company Ltd.
Castle House, 75/76 Wells Street, London W1T 3QT

1 2 3 4 5 6 7 8 9 0

For
  my mother

ACKNOWLEDGMENTS

Grateful acknowledgment is made to the editors of the publications in which these poems (or earlier versions) first appeared:

Alabama Literary Review: "Midas' Pause," "Laurel," "Woman in Front of Firelight," "Death and Transfiguration of a Star," "Jellyfish," "At the Church of Santa Prassede," "Restoration"

Bat City Review: "A Waterfall"

The Cincinnati Review: "Suggestive Grove," "The Climb"

Image: "At the Church of San Crisogono," "At the Church of Santa Maria Novella"

Literary Imagination: "Dark Ages"

Measure: "Leaving Saint Peter's Basilica"

Michigan Quarterly Review: "The Kingfisher"

The New Republic: "Chimes"

Ninth Letter: "Belltower," "Evening at the Dix"

Quadrant (Australia): "Erratics," "The Fish," "The Glass Sponge," "Geometry," "Another Sea Scene," "Io"

Raritan: "A Cove," "Shell," "Farthest Flame"

Salmagundi: "Snow Covering Leaves of a Magnolia," "Second Song," "Safe Swimming"

Southeast Review: "Anatomy of a Skylark," "Hadean Time," "Helioseismology"

The Southern Review: "Gullet," "Intoxication at Carmel-by-the Sea"

Southwest Review: "The Iceberg," "Field." "The Iceberg" won the Elizabeth Matchett Stover Award for the best poem published in its pages in 2002.

Verse Daily: "Grackles"

Virginia Quarterly Review: "Woman Reading to the Sea," "On Not Using the Word 'Cunt' in a Poem"

West Branch: "Grackles"

"Anatomy of a Skylark," "Chimes," and "Disobedience" were set to music by composer Steven Burke for *Songs from Bass Garden,* a song cycle for soprano and chamber orchestra performed by Susan Narucki and the Norfolk Chamber Orchestra at the 2005 Yale Summer Festival of Music.

I would like to thank the American Academy in Rome and the American Academy of Arts and Letters for the John Guare Rome Prize Fellowship, which enabled me to write many of these poems. Special thanks as well to John Hollander, Les Murray, Franco Mondini-Ruiz, Steven Burke, Saskia Hamilton, Jill Bialosky, Joyce Carol Oates, my students and colleagues at Centre College, and especially my husband, Philip White.

CONTENTS

3 *(Restoration)*

Woman Reading
to the Sea

1

With snow for flesh, with ice for heart,
I sit on high, an unguessed sphinx
begrudging acts that alter forms;
I never laugh—and never weep.

—Charles Baudelaire, "Beauty"
(translated by Richard Howard)

Gullet

Gnarled vision: a dark fist
rooting among the branches for ripe berries,

like a body of black starlings whose gold beaks
break and split into a clatter of knives

in neighborhood air.
I hear them interrupt the hour.

Wings, spiked feet, and oval bodies
slice through dogwoods' thin, scarred boughs

as they leave and light,
the rose-tipped, drooped, decrepit leaves

shuddering—.
The feathers on their backs

spell tapestries of birthing stars,
a cosmos carried.

It is no longer solid, the thing
that would be grabbed and preyed upon,

the thing imagined.
It loses color, becomes

something other than what they saw,
since what they see they take.

Sporadic flare of yellow mouths—
this other fruit

glanced among the color-weeping branches.
They're after berries,

red-orange orbs, persimmon constellations
in the Keatsian nest.

Not spirit, but bulk, pure matter
whose greed disrupts and shatters

whatever's picturesque.
It's divide, land, shake, plumb, pluck

and swallow. A red orb flashes against a yellow
beak, black gap, before the entrance shuts.

I like to watch that part—
take satisfaction in the berry's

roundness as it's caught in pointed lines
before the bird's head tips

to roll it back.
Each berry was a beauty

for some gullet to transform.
They are seekers flying over

fields I know, whose dry, sharp grasses
and weeds puncture the air

under their flight.
They are kin of my tongue, and thievish, and late.

Erratics

*Boulders caught in slow-moving glaciers
and carried along with the ice.*

Around you, this cold mother tongue
trundles without acknowledging
your single presence, dredges chunks
of landscape, troughs great peaks to junk
and sediment, carries you along.

One of the stubborn elements,
one of the ancient wholes gone wrong,
you're just a speck. This pale, cold mother
buries you in her enclosure
of locomotion, her slow lunge

of transparent cavalry. You can't loll
freely inside her, but are rolled
into the stampede of sameness. Dawns
wash blue and violet on her mass
in which frail, muted daylight drowns

through layers of muffling ice. You're pulled
hundreds of miles, for centuries,
trapped in a blank cocoon that cracks
branch slowly in, and re-fuse later.
Her sound is a chorus of fractures. Glass

shatters to veins, black roots. Whole chambers
echo with splintering. When melting
comes it will be the liquid gasp
of adamant impressions loosed
and streaming from you as you catch

on land, too heavy to budge farther.
Headed toward open sea, as ice
will do when its voice becomes less groan,
more supple, that which must abandon,
at last she leaves you: upright and alone.

Woman Reading to the Sea

after a painting by Franco Mondini-Ruiz

There's a certain freedom in the long blue slant
of its uncaring, in the wind that knocks
the surface onto rocks, and there's a dent

made in that wind by the woman who recites
straight into it, pretending the waves might hear
or that some larger being that is *sea*

or *seeing* hangs there listening, when sea air's
so clearly full of its own gusts and grunts,
inanimate uprisings. In the line

of no one's sight, her voice lost in the spray,
she feels a chilling freedom: how the foam
edges the sheets of zigzag patterned water

while gulls' shrill outbursts punctuate the sky
(one cloudy, sentimental phrase
or canvas brushed with amber, green, and rose).

What welcomes, and ignores, and doesn't question?
Sheer emptiness. It's like a husk
for her alone. It's like a shell for absence.

Without an audience, she makes a noise
swallowed by waves and wind, just as
the waves themselves—or no, just like the drops

lost in the waves, which neither care nor keep
distinctions—sweep out a place
inside an amphitheatre she imagines

rising around her, with columns that crash
instantly, like the white foam that collides
and shreds its layered castles. Her words drift,

dissolve, and disappear. A crest
of words has surged and poured into the sea.
It doesn't matter now what the lines say.

On Not Using the Word "Cunt" in a Poem

Certainly there's pressure to perform
in such a way what doesn't sound so stately
and isn't safe: *Let it be shorn,*

the poem's lush holiness. Let locks be trimmed.
Cut to the chase. How unchaste can you be?
Can I proffer a different kind of tongue,

one that licks nether regions? Can I start
offering words that aren't courtly or cute
and don't contain such blanket recanting

of words I use when I am in a wreck
or mad at somebody or being fucked
—those anti-canticles I chant when hurt,

the kind of words I punt when breaking glass
or bumping ceilings? Can I be curt,
not hunt for language so gosh-darned appealing

but pick what's more intransigent
and less ornate? Or is that just a judgment
ignorance can make—that stealing

the spotlight, showing one can "rough it up"
is really more mere decorativeness,
like the performance of a burlesque romp

by someone who would rather keep her dress?
Is that all poems can do to snatch attention,
use such dim tents of tricks? Let's nick

this baby in the bud: am I too mendicant
to fluid cadence? Do I serve lip
by thinking a poem is holy, not a hole

to thrust things in, for the very sake of thrusting?
Or do I suit myself for an audience
by shirking my naked voice, or the cliché

of what a woman's naked utterance
would be, as if just honest women cussed?
Should I be someone who docks elegance

because it's penal territory,
someone who takes the name of poetry
in vain—who kicks the ass of beauty?

I know we're all voyeurs, but can't
you come for me a different way this time
and listen, for one minute, to a poem

that's not revealing crotch and pay attention?
Is it impossible for me to strut
my stuff without the madonna/whore

dichotomy? Without the flash of tit
-illation, would you give my poem a date?
Or must I count my kind of cunning out?

Snow Covering Leaves of a Magnolia

Perfection stills, admits nothing,
like these white grains cupped and blinding
in lilac light—.

What its object "feels,"
if feeling's relevant,
is weight, the burden of surprise,

an iced admonishment
of months coming to fruit
on the vagrant summer's dark green

lustrous skins.
Nostalgia's excess
has been banished.

The new reign's virgin syllables,
in papery increments,
whisper their descent:

This is what you must turn to.
This zeroed sensation.
This blow to sprawl.

Horizons frozen
by a yield of white.
Growth is not virtue.

So the body becomes a statue
in puritan dress.
Nothing to do but stand there

and bear it, revoked,
while perfection lands each earnest
inimical stroke.

Eurydice

Why was delight not afraid?
               It meant inattention

or it meant new attention:
               a fish scale, scintillant,

limning deep deaths
               of color that formed an abyss . . .

A fish scale!
               —Junk lit

in ambiguous channels
               like symbolic gold leaf.

It meant a wrought
               and petalled land,

the sky's blue smoke
               over fields of asters,

years turning their soil
               into semaphores,

stamens, fibrils
               more intricate as you lower

your face to their details
which nearly speak.

Delight had an afterward
unseen, a figure

left behind, a trick of furtherance:
it was partial

and whole-blind.
It carried a little cavity

like belief
which meandering could fill.

Midas' Pause

I tried to ornament my life
with gold unfoldings, luteous curls

like antique horns and old illumined scrolls,
mosaics in an emperor's bath, or temple

hearths where virgins guarded aureate fires,
those pyres Aeneas piled high for the dead.

I wanted brilliance spooling from my fingers
as brown sprigs burst to floral springs,

to leave gilt in the dust each time I turned
away, and glister venerable trails

like the sheen of an exotic snail
streaming across the underworld,

fine threads of my bestowal. The gods
would not be more admired than I

with each branch of my royalty,
whatever I touch exploding—now—with value

new to itself, no longer just itself,
rare fingertips' bequeathal! Could I guess

embellishing the plain, my precious vice,
would leave me starved for what is ordinary,

would leave *us* ruined, whoever shared
a meal with me, whoever I might hand

a thing, or lay a palm on, kindly, warmly?
I can make a surface glitter. But I can't

drink or eat. No ladle of river water,
no crumb of bread or ripening autumn fig

brushes my lips before it strikes like lead,
each bruising gulp a new coin in the void

of my stomach, a hoard of grandeur
harder to bear each hour, undigested

and contrary to flesh. I languish
for the lack of what seems common: a tomato,

a simple root from a clump of musky soil,
my wife's familiar breath. What worth is worth

if it closes me from life? I lower myself
to the floor and watch the awful beauty

creep in circles radiating out
from where I sit, making a sound

of cracks and splits as it transfigures tiles
like a fleet of molten serpents lashing

from my still-lumpish flesh along
the floor into the blooming garden

where my wife bends now, clipping vines . . .
I see her gesture slowly as she sees

—too late—the alteration climb
from soil to overtake her body's standstill,

a metamorphosis that kills
as adders' poison does. She can't escape

without ripping her leg from her own ankle,
and so must freeze there, horrified,

as it crawls to fossilize her flesh,
her sex, her mother's milk

and then—slowly, at last—entraps
the small pulse of her throat, stopping her breath,

her mind that still beats tinnily in its cage
till all thought's wings are smothered . . .

But I move too fast, imagining that which
hasn't happened yet. Why does what weighs

in the hand and gleams before my sight
turn into a tyrant? How I want

to take one soiled and gardening hand
of hers from the dirt and kiss it! She absorbs

what light falls on her body, doesn't glow
as cold and as unfeeling as my opus.

Laurel

after Bernini's Apollo and Daphne

The man leaped lightly through the fields,
an arm's length from my heels. I felt my feet

burning, lifting bits of wrenched grass—chunks
of dirt, pebbles, root clumps—as I lunged past

where I had been, each former green harbor
abandoned. Air rasped in my ears,

whirred through the bristling foliage
that crowded my path, sent out spikes

and appendages. Twigs and leaf edges
scraped me, drew stuttering lines on my skin.

Through the blurred, varying canopy
I glimpsed a sky riven to pieces, slivers

of its blue patina like a broken vase,
the thing I'd looked up to, all its shapes

wasted; soft, blowing forms—horns and sheep
and goats, billows of noble cloth, bridal veils

—marred by the dimming fringe
overhead. Shadows and light climbed

my skin as if witted, racing over
flesh to some end—but what was it—

complete blinding white, like a temple?
Darkness of Persephone's throne?

Little bits of both flecked my path: broken
poses, scattered fundaments.

Each pound of my heels struck like needles.
Each foot dribbled blood

but I kept pushing, through one scrim
of branches to another, arriving

somewhere that was only on the way
to more evasion. I ran toward *me* from his

outstretching hands, a me that bloomed
in the distance, as if my self were the goal

all along. I heard him call:
Apollo. He pounded and glowed

behind me, his name flung through the narrow
scope of our flights, the air filled

with leafy ligatures and long, strangling vines.
I follow. He drove me from groves

calling "sister," "sister," "beloved"
as he flattened the fields. I looked behind me

to see the gold-spattered skin
of a god, smell the fragrance of honey

—too rich, too cloying, reminding me of bees,
a swarm I witnessed when I was a girl:

all momentum and hum
and restless needlings: a thunderous colony

of bodies: cacophonous wings.
I had been sitting on a log, had moved away

and then seen them: exactly in the place
my body had been a few seconds before

as if to inhabit the air still rich
with my breath—as if my previous presence

formed a portal, a sudden arch
for arrival. It was like this with Apollo:

each place I'd been was opening to him
even as my steps fled, the air emptied of me

ripe for his existence. Escape
belonged to me, and he wanted that too.

Apollo, the cloying smell:
the pound and call: his want. I hoped

the landscape would bury me,
that I could slip into the background,

as if into relief, the flat place
around those outstanding ones, icons raised

on white portals. *Father, father, protect me . . .*
Then the bark gnarled up between our limbs.

Then the hair he craved coiled to leaves.
He supposed me a surface, like a river

he could embark on, a fleet of waves,
silvery and involving . . . reveries

I hindered or interrupted, snapping fresh
tendrils midstretch. Now we are caught

like two stones. I wrench into branch,
my nerves numbed. An umber rush

floods my skull, and my mind
dulls and hardens, entrenched

with gold sap. Clenched, but freed.
Dropped questions, dropped fluidities—

The clefts in my hands splay to leaves. White
roots from my toes pierce cold ground.

No man will pry loose this body.
No god will wrack what is mine.

Suggestive Grove

These trees strike me as musicians, bent
toward one another's notes: one leans
to catch a strand of melody or the refrain

strummed on a mandolin. One hunches
vigilantly, displaying, with clenched silence,
that he'll be joining soon. One to the left

gestures to the rest to urge them on,
claps his hands and nods in duple time.
I see their creviced faces, how they mark,

without a word, the supple indications
intimate to them, or linger, poised,
as if this were about attentiveness

instead of making noise. Maybe it is—
just an intense abstraction, as they sway
in unison, or crane to hear new strains

begin, to understand what has begun
so they themselves might enter. Something
like faith encompasses them all,

something like faith or piety. They can't
conceive of ending it. One's shift
or surge of merging notes belongs

to each of them, was part of all their thoughts
about the notes before they played a song.
To improvise is contemplation's voice.

Woman in Front of Firelight

after a painting by Franco Mondini-Ruiz

This was a different light, but still familiar.
She felt illumined and she felt afraid
—serpents of color lashing through degrees

of ambience, heat. She knew their streams would fade
to ash, that their beauty would decompose,
like a passion that blazed into display

then dwindled, and there was a little sadness
to this hard truth: she lived in a world
where such lush burnishings arrayed

only a moment before they smoldered.
But now, enfolded in a pause
of orange flamboyance, even though its cause

was material, finite (unlike feeling),
she felt her life drawn through her eyes
toward some liquid body, rimmed in wings

beating and beating, that would not lower her
down to time. There were many things
outside this room she should remember,

that she should be turning in her mind
for these kindled minutes, golden, rare . . .
but thoughts left as she watched the fire.

Intoxication at Carmel-by-the-Sea

There was a wish to alter consciousness.
—Of course, there always was. We poured
half orange juice, half Beefeater, in two glasses,

pinched our noses and quickly gulped it down.
The mixture in our throats and bellies burned
then shifted to a silvery smooth glow

that radiated through our hands and faces.
That was the sweet part. But the rest was sour.
(For years I couldn't stand the smell of gin.)

Experience was our experiment.
We snuck out my low window to meet boys
and loll around the unlit, empty town,

down to the sea, if we had time to spare.
Its slosh of blue, its steady, vagrant hum,
mirrored our own inexact momentums.

At thirteen years, my grades were plummeting
but life had opened up, to people, air,
and landscapes tugging me from home like tides.

The gin thing didn't last. Intoxications
one after another were identified,
tested and tossed. What moves me, from this distance,

is how we fell so hard for everything
that drew us in: the pure, straight sentiments
driving our actions, even to stupid risks.

We were unused to being tentative,
the careful step. Yes. I remember most
that spirit of our trying, which is lost.

Horizontally, I Moved

I let my raw voice rise
but I was chastised, asked to hold my tongue.

I couldn't see the scenery for wings.
What good is blocked out paradise?

And hour after hour to hear that
pallid music: dull, facetious

words repeated to the same
sweet harmonies, like the manna that rained

constantly to feed us.
—I was bored. I tore a feather from one wing

and laid it on his throne, blood tipping
the quill. God found the trifle

and spent light rifling feathers to detect
a spot of loss. So I confessed:

I'd pulled it out for no good reason
except my discontent. He threw me

violently into chaos. Wracked with soot,
my lush wings locked;

now I could only lower myself slowly
and sink until I glimpsed reflected rays

in one thin strand of river through the garden.
This seemed a lasting shape

so I chose that for my seduction's
body: sinuous bolts with skin like waves

of water. Horizontally, I moved.

2
Hadean Time

It seemed, now seems, a boundless continent
Dark, waste, and wild, under the frown of Night
Starless exposed, and ever-threatening storms
Of Chaos blustering round, inclement sky;
Save on that side which from the wall of Heaven,
Though distant far, some small reflection gains
Of glimmering . . .

—John Milton, *Paradise Lost*

Hadean Time

The old stars exploded
and a grave new light began to form
in accretions of dust,
their metalled leavings.

Things broken and molten tumbled
uncontrollably, collided with the stars'
lost pillars at varying speeds. The initial
burst at the center faded.
By emptiness, some was consumed.

There was a big breather.
There was a time of great reduction,
of tossed and dismembered stuffs

and the frail light turned on itself,
folding inward, destroying most all
of its mass. It could have disappeared.

Then a huge flare fueled
by near-destruction rosed the ruins.
Scatterings of the old order,
once dispersed, drew together
with pulses and contractions,
many surfaces, many directions.

After all these pressures,
amid much spouting of gases and smokes,
you remained, trailed by your past
through piecemeal space.

You were fresh still, too fresh to trust,
the globule of an exploded triumph
soft with failure, not strong enough to carry on.

You could have been nothing,
could have been merely a mistake.

The essences shifted. The liquids rippled.
To be flat or brilliant or in between—
Even fact, before everything happens,
has no firm shape.

Dark Ages

With the oldest bodies of light
we can see shreds of beginning matter,
what came before
there was any light at all

and, in that vast state
gusts of fog, mist, grayish gases
thinned to ribbons and strips
vaguely reigned. This was genesis
not quite free of her past.

When the earliest stars appeared
one by one, each illumined
clump and flame-hoard forged
a distant fate. Some
warmed awhile, then waned.
Some grew hot over time.
Some drew a molten fortune
from whatever lit remnants they could,
reeling faster. Some lost control
and flailed to fiery tentacles
clutching backward—they left visual shrieks.

Those with a future in emptiness
bulged from a self-scalding core
but rounded their own reactions
in the iron of perfect spheres.

Their blue-red lesser fires
brightened to white heat, white as an eye
looking out on terrain unknown,
still clouded. These were the eyes,
just opened, of the seer shocked
to recognize such distortion, such lack
of clarity. How much still to be done!

Thus chewing the matter over
another, and another, was born
in a chain of increasing vision.
Each new gaze broke the grayish drifts
afresh. The background shifted its bits,
the foggy veils dissolved
in widening rings of heat
as stars, suns, other brilliancies
(like eyes as well) resolved to burn.

Eventually, the seers cleared
this place of ambiguity
or portions of it. They made it an active black,
colder, but seeded with galaxies,
composed of bright and dark,
night and day.
There were chances for cosmic wrecks
but for substance too, and order.

Now, shreds of those first mists
occasionally pass
across the oldest source of light
more potent than a billion of our suns.

If we look hard and fast
we can see them.

Farthest Flame

Whatever you are comes from the sun.
It is useful to remember this
as you go around chasing days.

The sun is not round.
It appears so because its geometries are burning.
It cannot have a fixed shape
because its edges are lopped by flame.

Clipped, cut, carved in a moving margin
peaked with fluid fire. Fire that is no color.
Fire of such wild roil it kills the idea of color.
Fire the idea of which is only a beginning
to your mind and its elliptical frames.

This fire is your reason for being,
the reason itself, and in it nothing rests,
nothing lives or breathes
for millions and millions of miles.

The sun has many tongues
it flicks coarsely, it flicks loudly.
Its eruptions are violent, a violence its own change claims.

It can swallow its own disturbances
on a blistered surface curling to the core
yet send out signals through the cold of space
ending gently, many millions of miles away.

It has a light touch, this fevered origin
after, long after, it leaves the place
repetitive, terrible, where dark is eaten
again and again by panicked tongues,
where the fire and its tongues eat darkness.

The Iceberg

The iceberg moves will-less
through shades of gray and gray,
a tower of clouded glass

seeming proud of isolation, rising
in air. Or the iceberg's top lies
flat along the water, its misshapen

turrets jutting below the surface
like an upside down, Gothic cathedral
made of ice.

Around the tower and its moat
or the inverted iceberg, or tipped cathedral
dipped in the green-black liquid and remote

in mists (if you could stand in the middle
of it all) is the smell of ice and brine,
rough sea in the purist wind

that blows from far-off coasts
and stays here, freshening.
You would taste a tinge of time

on your tongue, its encrystalled distances
jagged in the strong stark absence of lament—
that chunk of knowledge always inaccessible

but always defended by the physical
world, without judgment or pretense,
simply floating.

Death and Transfiguration of a Star

Ambitious beam,
what's physical in your case "strains
all concepts of the conditions
of matter." Trillions of times
strict as steel, thousands the pull

of the earth's magnetic field,
spinning and spinning
on mercurial impulse
as if in a race to defeat
only your past increase, earlier

your inner center became your cloak
in a brash refashioning,
your deepest matter worn now on the sleeve,
old metals polished,
a world of sword blades clashed

a millisecond. What's physical
in you swells beyond mere image. Numbers pale.
Surface "smooth as a billiard ball"
won't cut it. Pre-intellectual,
dependent on the mind

to be imagined but not to exist,
after the ultimate solipsist-
ic meltdown—all guns in the arsenal
for despair, all hooves in the stable
of soldering force,

all shards of the heavenly mirror
held in your fists—you stabilize
instead of disappear,
your silver arms stretch light light-years
ahead of dying.

Some hole awaits
as blackness must
the most boggling volts. You will be
zero volume, endless density,
when words don't leave a trace.

The Fish

How they appear: tunneled vision
in a brackish world. But they weave through it,
ambient, loose as the drops that brush their skin,
slick colony of mists. Or do not weave.

These snaking vines, these luminous passersby
who quiver and blink in strange upstagings
don't form obstructions to a path, but mark details
in an intimate landscape, one that, though vast,
in practice is always narrowed . . .

Minutiae abound, things small as the tip
of an eyelash, which the fish might gulp,
for inside lies the way to another world
of blood, fanned bones, cold pearly spears
around which scales furl armor. Slits
for breath, sleek passageways, flutter life
in beats, the rhythm of their keeping.

Where they exist: this pulse they are hinged on,
this harsh gill music. In colorless fog,
or where a billion hues confound,
they can settle on the island of that
breathing, hold fast to the stone of it
as the great mouth churns, each wave
one ring of truth the sea itself extends.

Jellyfish

Movement means closure,
a thrust from where you are,
that gelid other plane,

your bell-like head
with wordless aperture
emptying, emptying,

the pleats of your innards,
a shallow accordion.
Your tendrils trail neon

lit cities of cells
—you, pellucid ferry,
invisibly carried

spun dome like the ghost
of some merry-go-round.
And we who don't float

with such unconscious ease
think it terror to rise
from our notions of *land*,

rock, and *ownership*, can't
ride a bottomless plain,
colored trust in our sails,

in the lax, placid matter
that holds, not from falls
(for you too fill your head

so your gossamer motors
move onward) but holds
your shape firm. Even you,

if you never once moved,
if you didn't take in
the first place where you are,

fold around that cold present
then push out, with liquid
momentum (like knowledge)

from flushed, chambered cells,
would ascend nowhere new.
In the planktonic dark,

a touch is the world,
the devouring of touch
motion's guidance. Your emptied

bell head tolls the thrust,
the sole luminous effort—clear
life thinking's lost!

Anatomy of a Skylark

Inside a bird there are
chambers and chambers,
tunnels through scapular
bones, tarsus flues.

Tongue under mandible
thin, flat, and tapered.
Feathers in mantle top
down-folded wing.

Oxygen circulates
pale pair of lungs,
paths to esophagus,
gizzard and heart

(thumbnail-sized). Breast, of course,
puffed up with plumage,
quills the original
pinpointed art.

Words follow from this.
Do they say anything
mythic as music
while lizard feet cling?

Instruments grew in
the hollow where noises
—genus of throat—
found a painstaking form.

The Glass Sponge

Pheronema carpenteri

Your body housed inside a nest of glass,
its lucid needles woven
in radiant networks like a dozen
webs of spiders sewn into a dome
and coated with a layer of liquid quartz
so that they are fixed as crystal
around that softness which the sea flows through,
that softness full of holes.

Cascades of glass twist down
to rope you to the sand. Or
one potent spike of glass stabs the sea floor
to lock you in that dim frontier
where you will shine in the eye of a traveler,
sucking in food and releasing wastes
through your spiked and greedy osculum.

Human divers may loose your root,
unhook it carefully (for your edges cut)
and lift you to the land-locked world where sun
shrivels your body to dust
and dries the needles of your shell
to be sold, a dazzling valuable
tourists misapprehend
as the work of a minor craftsman.

A Waterfall

Starting at the pinnacle,
ice-held and wind-whipped,
threading through the solid planes of years,

caught now in pits, now caves, now eddies
of froth like lace or quiet muddied pools,
making its way from ordered lines to whorls,

down gutters other, older flows have wrought
in fossiled rock, inscribing them with grit
and vestiges, to finishes unknown

at bottom, long lax lake or stifling dam,
fishless or filled with tadpoles, algae, trout
—whatever stops the overarching flow's

mysterious course is not for me
to guess; each slip of tongue and shining length
and glassy skein that swings from bank to bank,

slaps into dark obstructions, crashes, breaks,
and hurtles, faster waters at its back
turns into sounds: a low, insistent drawl

of water rippling slow to cross a wake,
the high cries when it hits the hardest rocks
or bursts into a fan of foam in air,

the minor murmurs, major fluted leaps
in choral pairs, the wavering water strings
looped over crannies, tightened on thin stones

while underneath, a range of lower notes
now integral, now hidden, harbored, drawn,
withdrawn, or pulled to fuller pools below

before it mingles, rises, circles, falls
continually; and of the lofty height
where it began, that iced and thin-aired peak

I started from, I can't hear anything:
the wellspring's real, just as the finish is
but from right here, those seem like vision, silence.

The Kingfisher

I wanted to see a kingfisher
with its throat bound up in whiteness
and its black crest aimed at clouds.

I didn't know what it looked like,
not really. In poems and stories
it would flicker, a subtle omen.

But a kingfisher appeared
one February Sunday.
First, a high, rattling call

like a constant shake of maracas.
Then the bird itself touched down
on an aged tree, on a pond's island,

in a circle of melting ice.
From that one place, it called and called
and its call tapped a contradiction

to the cold, a noise that loosened
the ice's thin sheets.
The kingfisher lifted its tail

up and down, moved close to the water,
moved closer. Its eyes skimmed the pond.
I clumsily focused binoculars:

the white throat, the angular crest!
—perceptible, barely, by color
and form, a lot like a painting

viewed so close up it's blurred.
Step away. Step away. I didn't
from my life's one mention of kingfisher

until some noise
(a rifle, or muffler, or tree fall
in the distance) triggered its flight

and then I watched it lift
—it's heavy, a bird more burdened
than some, and not all grace—

trailing calls like the beads of a rosary:
a string of clicks in air,
a shadow leaving the ice.

Evening at the Dix

Looking into the river at dusk, I noticed
nothing but the silver waffling common
to the water's face if there were wind. But then
I heard strange slapping sounds. Was there a tide
that rose and lapped the limestone banks?
Of course there wasn't; this was just a river.
I leaned over the bridge to look more closely.
Because of the lean, late rays of sun
that poured into the river like a flashlight
I could see straight through the water's haze:
In the dull shallows under the bridge
a school of minnows turned to hang one
slant direction from another, their bodies
flickering greenish bronze. I raised
my eyes and saw the river's face
disturbed with rings right on the surface
that burst and disappeared. These made the sounds
I had heard: The long, lithe bodies of the bass
writhed up so their back fins just broke
the water, then slipped back into the murk.
One place and then another would be touched
so the effect—in that gold, nostalgic light—
was of a syncopation, like the notes
played on a piano, how one finger strikes
and sinks into a silent drift just as
another note is played. It happened quickly,
my noticing, the river dabbed with circles,
the circles met and pierced by curving fish,
slick, scaled, with dull-gazed eyes

and torsos long, in the muddy veils, as eels.
The river seemed to reveal itself, all fins,
tails, mouthparts, pushing themselves through
the fibrous threshold of its currents, a world
drawn open to this watery vein
in which things flailed. Three great blue herons
floated across the river, angling wings.
A motor boat skirred up the water.
The herons arced away. The bass fell quiet.
The waterline diminished with the light.

Another Sea Scene

Yes, the sunlight glitters on the water
as it has before, as it will again.
Your seeing it this way can hardly matter.

You are one of millions, like those azure threads
warping and weaving the surface of the water,
drawing themselves in ripples over matter,

unraveled by the wind. The gulls mock
you. They squawk, *Her seeing does not matter.*
Squawk! As they swoop through air again.

They've seen one person here after another.
The sun still glimmers and it has no aim
besides this sluggish crawl on land and water,

the water clearly azure near the shore
where cliffs hang, where the coves are sheer.
Above the waves' azure shifts, gulls' wings aim

only to catch wind drifts. The water
under them glitters, glitters again,
transparent stuff somebody else has seen.

Field

Is it a thing we build inside ourselves
that gives us so much purpose? Maybe.
But sometimes, when I look out on a field
as others did, have done—at chicory's
angular slants of blue, bull thistle's
bursts of purple fervor, Queen Anne's lace,
and all the other pigments of expanse
—tall, weedy flourishes
that nudged into black atmospheres
their leaf, or sprout, or semaphore,
stemmed inch by green stemmed inch, and wove
a length of knots and stoppages that filled
the land's flat vacancy—my thought
seeps back into itself, under a grid
of soil and pale curved roots, as if
the mind were just another naked field,
the darkened mind.

Grackles

They were not one body. Yet they seemed
held together by some order, their thick necks
flickering with a blue-black iridescence,
their yellow-circled pupils bright and cold.

In a wave of differences that passed
low over the surface of my yard,
they picked it clean of morning's fritillaries
and other summer gestures fall discards

then settled on the hill behind the fence
for several teeming minutes to remark
its tapestry, each razored beak, each tail
parting Sunday's gray air like a spear.

I could tell you that they gathered up
the darkness of my winter thought that day
in mid-September, bundled it, black-ribboned,
into sleek coats and lifted it from me

just as you have imagined. But this
would be a lie. I watched them comb the fields
with interest, and, when their beak's clicks had died,
turned back to what I was.

Chimes

Leaves flutter wild in wind.
Now, as day descends,
he hears the old wind chimes.

Moon like a portal shines
through nearby trees again.
Wind plays on the chimes.

His neighbors' lights go on
—gold from the windowpanes.
A fence and garden dims.

All matter must succumb,
he thinks, as darkness climbs.
Houses lose their lines.

Still, the old wind chimes
play in the air again,
a tune without a mind.

Shell

There is almost no wind.
The river's surface shines but is barely moving.
Two mink slip into the blue-green

dusky water from a limestone shelf.
It took me a long time to arrive here
with an emptiness like a hollow snail shell

which this river water perfectly fills,
though the shell was crafted for a certain body
as our brains seem crannied for belief.

Since I have no belief, I must look
very carefully. I must be devoted and scraped clean
of my lavish concepts. I must prepare

a baptism for the absence of faith.
The water's shallows will swallow its breath
like a dying animal's, until it is drubbed and quiet.

Nothing now but the runnels
on the river's surface, the mink's slide
in siltish depths, an orange fish flexing in air

for a second so the eye sees one emergence
vivid and detached out there
after I have made Him disappear.

3

Restoration

The great mouths of the god's house, thunderstruck,
Will never open till you pray.

—Virgil, *The Aeneid*
(translated by Robert Fitzgerald)

Thou stranger, which for Rome in Rome here seekest,
And nought of Rome in Rome perceiv'st at all . . .

—Joachim du Bellay
(translated by Edmund Spenser)

Leaving Saint Peter's Basilica

It isn't only the marble, the tombs of bronze,
the rigid brilliance of the angled stones,
the columns lined with purpose, glossed with time.

It's the shadow across the palm of someone's hand,
the action stopped: the folds of angels' robes
forever folded, the outstretched arms of popes

who supplicate or bless or mouth a prayer
with static, gesturing limbs. It's all the layers
hidden from us, the dust that's flesh entombed,

the sculptures of the women looking down
and one of two great lions, claws unsheathed
—vigilant, though their stone eyes look on nothing.

And last and least, it's me hunched on a pew,
scribbling to the light of burning candles,
trying to hide the sacrilege of writing

from all the other watchful bodies here,
those hardened into statue and those moving
steadily, until they trickle out

from the confines of the church. Sublime
extravagance, we find it, as we exit
into the portico and out the doors,

putting some space between it and ourselves
until the dome reappears, its arcs aglow,
the dusk-lit clouds around it pinkish white

and drifting past in gilded lumps like stucco
or bodies of other angels, selves, contorted,
rapturous, and—finally—dissolved.

At the Church of Santa Prassede

In the Chapel of the Garden of Paradise
(Rome)

Heaven would be dull compared to these
panes and flecks of color

curving over us—.
Every surface covered.

Every surface jewelled.
Coral and jade. Turquoise, topaz, agate.

More succinct than paint,
these glassed, transcending hues.

From the smallest scale they widen
into landscapes more intense

than we imagined, obliterating
even the idea of sin, and creating

a realm that we can look to from our realm.
Who cares if there is no window, no sun,

no home like this dreamed mosaic
except in memory?

Who cares about the doorway
(which must be entered) to a dimmer world

or that there is nothing
of our language rendered clearly,

when there is this vision made entirely
of particles assembled,

which didn't arrive?
See how the eye moves

from cut, shimmering square
to cut, shimmering square,

each increment's aspect placed
(like the flecks of an insect's scale)

by hands that have disappeared?
How it matters that those hands have disappeared?

At the Church of Santa Maria Novella

(Florence)

There is nothing to hold me.
The marble floor is bare and hard.

The buttressed ceiling seems to swim
with coldest gusts—.

From one end of the church, a burst
of piped-in choral music—Handel,

or is it Mozart? In tinny jubilation,
the voices of exuberance

pour from the candlelit apse.
A group of tourists pauses

before this church's masterpiece,
Masaccio's *Trinity*, their guide explaining

the precise new view arranged
by the deceptively painted panels

the artist contrived: there,
Masaccio created a room or temple

for Christ's crucifixion, "an example
of the Renaissance's first linear

perspective." And here,
the false recesses of Masaccio's chamber

contrast with the marble floors
and columns of the church that appears

so impermeable our flesh might slip
away from it, might fall and shatter.

Masaccio's fresco holds Christ
against the slick, flat surfaces like bones

that do not hold a thing:
a corridor inside a temple

inside a room of time,
a place where he can hang

in our glance, an invented embrace.
God stands behind Christ,

a white dove on his chest.
God's cloak is a cloud of dark blue.

He appears to support Christ
in his suffering

but that blue cloak billows
as if it were made of emptiness,

of cold and multiplying space.
Christ's cross will tip back

and his body, barely fastened to it,
will tear through that thin, fading layer

of the artist's color, tumble back
to a blackness that plummets

beyond surface, through a distance
without memory, without stars,

without God's voice. And he
will have to suffer that falling.

At the Church of San Crisogono
(Rome)

I'm hanging around the outskirts of the altar.
Entra! the custodian tells me, sweeping his hands,
and hesitant to step up there, I do:

What strikes me first is the long aisle
that spreads from where I stand through the expanse
of the church's hollow. Like a theater's

stage the apse gives me a different view
from what I thought I'd seen, a backward view:
I see where people seat themselves to listen.

I see the path that leads them to the pews
but don't see what's on either side, and don't
catch any of that whorled maze of mosaics

that crown and background me (or who would speak
from here). The baldachino's columns
gleam with faint slant lines of light.

I've glimpsed a lot of gold-encrusted rooms
with radiant digressions on each side
and lavish, painted chapels, but I think

the best place for god-worship is like this:
a narrow rectangle, a room plain and severe
so no one loses focus, with authority

above, and awe boxed in below.
In a pew by an effigy, a beggar woman
with a cloth around her head sits, bends, and bobs

as she mutters to her Christ. Outside
the thunder cracks and splinters like a gun
(we came inside from violent morning rains).

Still up on high, I linger to one side
of the lectern, so my vision is askew,
but I don't want to bother honest worship

and I'm aware of my shoes that, trailing rain
and runoff from Rome's flooded cobblestones,
muck up the clear, delineated marble:

gray-green, white, and blue triangles and squares;
octagons, circles in circles, perfect forms
tucked and bound, eternally, it seems.

Out in the pews, another person prays.
He catches sight of me, but doesn't frown
or shake his head. How does he bear

us awkward, gawking tourists, who don't come
to worship, in his space? I step back down
and look behind the lectern as I do:

the dark wood-carved reliefs around the apse
show angel after angel with splayed wings.
For a century they've kept their length of silence.

The man who waved me in is locking doors
with clicking sounds. The woman leaves her pew
and kneels before the sculpture of the Virgin.

With high, insistent tones her phrases rise,
lilt and rise before red candles burning.
We enter rain to fragments of her pleading.

At the Church of San Pietro a Maella

(Naples)

In the distance, someone plays a piano
as I walk into the interior stripped
as bones, and see a woman weeping
in the first side chapel. She shields her face
with a hand to hide her eyes, her body
turned to one side on the pew, as if
only half of her were worshipping,
as if she might bolt at any moment.

The nave is simple, with keyhole windows
that admit ample light. An old crucifix
(Byzantine? medieval?) hangs on a wall
that crumbles, its scarlets and ochres soaked
into dark aged wood, their outlines softening.

Deep in the church, I discover something:
an abandoned chapel, a sort of homage
to neglect, dust-covered and shabby, with cobwebs
blocking the window, the once-vivid paint
of frescoes of saints turned gray on gray,
the fabulations of image worn down
without rescue. I touch the scenes, which are cold
and like palimpsests. The chapel's sculptures
are powdering, their edges adrift,
their wings and faces grotesquely broken.

The most truth I've seen, this rotting vision.
Also the most sad. No one has swept
out decay, held it back or at bay. When I'm done

with looking, I stand at the church's entrance
and absorb the impression. What's magnified
seems small, unsacred. And what is fading
is vastness—vastness built inside.

Then the clamor and hammering of Naples returns,
and the dingy sunlight, and market stalls
and brusque, rough gestures, and shadows that race
each minute, each step. In the church behind me
the old walls weep interminably
their vestiges of . . . history? faith? some
deeper crafting? It isn't a place
I'd seek for an ideal holiness
but it holds them well, I think: my world
and another world that disappears,
shedding its textures and its tints,
more fascinating and more clearly
what it never was than I imagined.

At the Church of San Clemente

(Rome)

Once more I've come to see what can be seen:
flashes of gold, a raised medieval choir
of ivory, tile in snaking patterns
that ravel and unravel on the floor.

It's winter. There's a damp, raw,
penetrating chill to all the marble
although the nave is lanced with whitish sun.
I see my breath beside the ancient columns.

Today, there are no real worshippers. All
are here for mere art's sake. Just well-
dressed tourists, scented, prosperous,
who wander, awed, or rest along the pews

so I walk down steps into the old basilica
whose chambers lie below street level
above an even older site of worship.
Instead of vibrant, gold-entwined mosaics,

here the frescoes graphing out the tales
of saints are losing hues before my eyes,
their actions seen in parts. The floor's
red surface has been almost walked away.

Down at the lowest level, after
visits to several mildewed, dusty rooms
(a bare bulb every ten feet lights the way),
I see something that strikes me as even stranger:

four doorways, one after another, each
the size of a person, keyhole-shaped rectangles
rounded at the top. I guess
it's not so strange, except they're cut in stone

precisely for a body to pass through
as many have for centuries by now.
I pass through every one of them,
my shadow gliding along uneven floors

in front of me, lumpish and black. Last
of all, as I'm set to ascend, I see
one cavern barred behind a grill
of iron at the bottom of the stairs, and stoop

to look inside: The light from where I stand
extends a little into that weird place
but then is sucked inside it, dwindling
in increments, until all I can tell

of the back, the very back of it, is blackness.
It's noon and the church must close. I climb
up into the brighter rooms as bells
begin: six rings, six more. And I emerge.

At the Church of Santa Cecilia

(Rome)

It is all about restoration
in the courtyard of the basilica

where a man in a white uniform scrapes
at the antique marble basin

in the middle of an empty fountain.
He wears a clear mask and a white hood.

His tool makes a high, keening sound
as it flays bits of dust from the past.

The fountain is surrounded by orange mesh
draped from red poles.

Inside, Cecilia will be all white,
coiled cold marble, her faced turned

from us all. I walk into the entryway
where cupids with distorted faces

and wreaths of fruit for halos soar on walls,
small painted puffs of cloth

covering their tiny penises.
Straight ahead, a mosaic of Jesus,

Mary, St. Peter, Cecilia, her husband Valerian,
and the jutting, crooked towers of holy cities

beside rows of faithful flocks, in Byzantine form
reflects some bits of celestial glory

through windows leaking meagre light.
Christ blesses them all with one raised hand.

The marble Cecilia lies as she was "found"
when they opened her tomb in 1599:

curled on one side, knees bent, wrists together.
Instead of her face, I see the shape of a small breast

under folds of thin cloth, the back of her neck
and the terrible executioner's gash

across her throat (a botched beheading
that did not, reportedly, kill her for three days).

The cloth wrapping her head
has slipped to show a few stray locks of hair.

She looks as if she has chosen to twist her sight,
has pressed her seeing hard into the ground.

As I walk back through the courtyard, I see
the restorer's face. *She* has unzipped

the top of her white suit a little (because
of the heat? For a little more freedom

of movement?). Her blouse under the white suit is red.
Several locks of hair fall forward

around the mask as she bends to her task
of chiseling, cleaning. I leave that whiteness behind.

Restoration

Decline is this blue dusk
sharp around the steeple
and a belltower's edge,

in which street lamps glow orange
and shoes clatter on cobblestones.
A person or two stops

to speak of what they know
while hurrying past, and I listen
to their words pry the weight of darkness.

Wholly anonymous,
I watch light sink into stones.
I watch alleys, baroque facades,

shop fronts and fountains all slide
toward decay, and I grip them with sight
—this medieval church, for example,

its chiseled, elaborate face.
Inside, I find shadows draped
in chapels and on marble tombs

but I wander until the lines
of the paintings and sculptures fade
so much I see the way out

alone. There's a little more light
outdoors, and I think of the church
left behind overspread with shadow

as I and the others leave,
of its hard and silent altar.
We restore the things we need

in mind; restore and preserve
with vision, or with fresh thought,
in passing only, the icons

established, not quite our own,
thus witnessed, and slightly altered,
as we walk through the holy city

(just as we move through a poem),
choosing what to let dim, what grace
with a transient inner light.

4

"The opposite [of death] is desire."

—Blanche Dubois in *A Streetcar Named Desire*
by Tennessee Williams

Maenads

It traveled over the tall gates of our gardens,
our threshold stones,

his song about something done,
gone, lost, a body not touched again,

not like our bodies. We made him reckon them:
receptive flesh—our flesh!—he left behind

as flashes through the forest's deformations
though he drew the animals near him

with that bodiless voice,
though even the trees leaned down,

even the stones crept close,
even the dead turned, groaned,

even Persephone,
half her life's light drained

—that wisp!—was pricked to sympathy.
Sepulchres quaked.

A ripple rocked the underworld's black veins
as a rain floods roots.

For something done,
for a girl who was far too simple,

who saw only a surface, not the peril
underneath, who ranged the fields

for loveliness, with a maiden's erring sight—
just this, and this,

not what unwinds below
the wash of flowers on the meadow's knoll.

Beyond the surface it is dark
and after you have seen it

you can't go back.
It was his clutched mistake,

the dream that slid out of his arms.
Should he blame the dream?

Her own delight in the meadow?
The hell, or world, that underscores delight?

The blame attached to nothing. But his voice
took shape. For years we listened,

trying to turn his sight. How ignorant!
He had no more a body for a woman

than stones did. He surrounded himself with boys
as if returns to boyhood

would yank him out of time.
—Yet his song was about a girl

he loved as skin and bones.
It maddened us

to sense the pool of feeling in his song
denied by flesh.

By the time we tore it from his voice,
his body had already vanished.

Belltower

My throat is a belltower
in a stone cathedral
tolled and echoing.

Great pangs of discord
plumb the hollow calm there
where once woolen blue

morning mist filled the arcs
of the belltower's walls
until gray doves awoke

in the soft down of hope,
of desire. Now the bells
peal all wrong, if an ear

could hear deep, muffled chords
from a tangled up throat
that feels like a belltower

rung wild with fear
by strong hands. But the bells'
tone belongs to no town.

Io

Because he is near
you constantly explode,
revealing the hidden liquid
at your center, a sort of fear

as he hangs there, his great density
anchoring storms,
the globe of his mass
clouded orange in your face.

Tides tied to this lord
of your lava, his appeal
makes you wobble. Your veneer
—the smooth body he longed for—

cracks, then spews out hot jets.
Now your molten heart shows
how a hard shell recovers
with soft, flooding depths.

Hades

(Persephone)

You who pulled me for your dark concerns
must know that I never

wished to be bound,
only taken. And because

overshadowing motion
awoke in you the near-dead coals

so they glowed, I would let you
consider me ember,

ghost with you through those ashen rooms
razed of abandonment,

comb lifeless pools
so deeply inclined. I would gladly

eat with you, touch, discuss
that land beyond your portals, filled

with the dumb and deceived,
venturing out only to prove

my barren preference.
—It was due to me. Plenty

could be had up there in the wrack
of shallows, while we distilled,

turning ourselves on ourselves
like figures in a forge

without light—.
We became more solid

by what we did not meet
in the tenebrous balm

of our element, the enduring gloom.
Our outlines sharpened. Charred

by a smoldering heat, we then cooled
so much that our bodies,

mistaken as husks,
flaked from their cores.

Disobedience

(Eve)

God, I belong to no one.
Not even one of your minions.

So when the strange man pinned
me against the bricks, drew my hand

to his crotch, I thought,
Good! Let Him watch.

Let Him see how I worship
on my knees. In an empty alley.

Let Him see how my lips
open and close to the profane ballet

of desire without a heart.
In these rough motions that start

from knowledge, let there be pleasure.
And when the young man pushed

my head down farther, slipped
himself into my voice,

when I felt the pristine statue
of my body tip and shatter

into many stones, I thought (again)
Good! It does not matter

that I break. It does not mean
I should not speak. I'm not a thing

to be defined, by Him, by any one.
I'm not a thing He orders.

I choose this prayer instead.
If I am afraid, I am afraid

of myself, or of another. Not of you.
Not of You, my absent Father.

Rapture's Lack

Why must lust
                depend on division?

Why does sex stun
                when it's most unbound?

To be whole, they have always told me,
                is the province

of a woman: to be full: fulfilled.
                Nothing about fear.

Nothing about the sublime
                writhed desire

locked in body and mind,
                the incapable aches

roiling sleep—.
                What spurs the blood

into simmering
                does not love it,

would not suffer one lack
                to prevent its being spilled.

What becomes one body
                to another

is imagining, not truth. How terribly
               this sort of rapture

—covetous, uncluttered—
                    cleaves us empty.

Geometry

I made myself a circle, then a square.
I made a box too small for him to open
and then a portal which, from anywhere,
displayed the magnitude of my affection.

Once full of pliant roundnesses and curves,
his private tapestry, I made a skin
tight as a drum, impervious to pain
and drew this on as if to stop an army,

then turned into a blossom on a plain,
rose-like and fragrant, luring him to come
and nestle in. I threw the flower at him
crumpled in a ball. It hit the floor

and there I was: plain angry red, a sphere
as foreign to his faculties as Mars.
In every way I wanted him to care.
I made myself a circle, then a square.

The Goddess Stopped

(Thetis)

In that grotto I would go to, shadows
rocked along the tufa walls

and low waves cradled out to sea
the bay's evening detritus. Sprawled

on a stone warmed by a ray that struck
its surface from a gap, I'd rest

until ready to enter the ocean depths
again. He saw me in that slash

of sun—was slinging his net of fish
back to another shore—dropped it, and crept

soft to my sleeping body to link his
arms around me. —Feverish heart

that pounded loudly! I woke to charge
at his hold, a heron with flapping wings

so strong they should have flung him.
He gripped hard. So I jerked upright,

a cedar tree with bristling needles
and scabrous bark—he held. I writhed

to a tiger, volcanic with tearing shafts.
He loosened and I slithered free.

—How could I be one self, yet so many?
Proteus counseled him, and when he came

a second time, as my shape ranged
from wrangling fins to brutal tufa jags,

he refused to weaken, though he bled
and burned from what flailed, lunged, or scraped.

No matter how she changes, keep
your grip. She will be what she was

eventually. Just wait. Proteus' words.
My last form was an icicle whose crags

thrust tips like blades. Peleus wept
at such concrete estrangements

but he stayed. By the time dawn flared
on the darkened tide, I couldn't bear

the weight of change any longer, shrank
to myself again. We slept. I dreamed

of the bay, its sickle shape held by the land
and when we woke, we conceived our Achilles.

Second Song
(1978)

First stacked heels, first gold hoops, first sexy
skirt, green and diaphanous wraparound

Danskin skirt meant for my ballet class,
first junior high school dance, first pulsing bulbs

and loud familiar music loosening limbs
to moves I'd only practiced with a girlfriend;

Does this look okay? Is this cool? Or dumb?
Not wobbling between confidence and shame.

Stabs of excitement walking in the gym
darkwashed from pristine bleakness to a den

of red light, strobe light, eleven and twelve year-olds
finding themselves, like me, in their new skins

of carnal creatures in a blurry realm,
a place that in our minds could writhe with vipers

or blaze with stars. We were the epic heroes
in an adventure just shoved off from shore

or else we were little specks inside a beaker
who'd rearrange, assimilate, and die.

First practice stopped, to lose track in the end
of how I wanted to look and begin moving

freely and indiscreetly to the BeeGees,
Marvin Gaye, Santana, the Eagles, Chic.

By song two, I'd wiped out all thought of home,
the port that, dazed and sweating, I'd return to,

a Persephone who wanted to stay with Pluto:
changed on the inside, ready to leave her mother

without a word or tear. I was that young
and unentrenched, first body's pull that strong.

Safe Swimming

Percy Priest Lake one July afternoon,
me in my bright orange life vest

and round, wide face, wearing a two-piece,
red with beige stripes.

The two of you sit in the motorboat and sip
canned beer out of an ice chest

so cold the aluminum drips.
Into the long, green, odorous wake

of the water, lukewarm and thick
with its summer spawning, its reek of live fish,

I drop my body, sleek and plump as a seal's.
The lake sheathes my skin, slips over and coats

my hair ends. Up close, the water's brown.
On the boat you sip your beer again

and laugh. I revise it now, a scene so crisp
nobody but myself has witnessed it

who's still alive: the clean, white motorboat,
the two of you leaning at ease, lightly dressed,

you laughing, tossing your lipsticked smile back,
your hair freshly set. It's the mid-1970s.

I'm a spark on this memory's surface,
its riveted warp; a watery sack of bone

and flesh, a red speck. I am six or seven.
After I swim, we will eat sardines

on crackers smeared with yellow mustard
so bright it seems leaked from the sun.

The two of you look happy in this light
I have captured. Now, you are looking at me.

I'm swimming—see? I'm close to the boat
where you are, but free to swing my vision

to the forested banks behind my head
that hold pockets of darkness, an infinite shimmer

of leaves. The Tennessee sunlight hammers
several feet of the lake to a warm, womb-like silt

that makes me sleepy. I should swim back.
But this day will last hours—we all can feel it.

It holds us in the palm of a leisure
so timeless it might still be here.

I am floating separate, but know your figures
are behind me, in the hold of what's stopped.

You laugh and talk. I could meet your eyes
from my point in near-distance. The boat gently rocks.

Helioseismology

The study of acoustic oscillations
that make the sun ring like a bell.

No hole at the center,
so how do you ring?

Surface oscillations
and low, thrumming waves

roll across you, or shudder
at your deepest range . . .

One need not be empty
to sound. You're the stop

in the cosmos's hollow,
the odd ball of particles

hung in the bell
whose gold dome, hammered fresh

and still smoking, lies stretched
far above us. The top

of this rounded container,
sloped down to a rim

I'll call wide open "lips"
brimmed with terrible ends

and beginnings, new clappers
of bronze, which will take

giant hold when you're gone
(they are forging already)

I can't—listening—see
being stuck in the dumb

middle dust of the gong-haunted,
unsettled chamber

between your last clang
and the vibrating dome.

The Climb

A crack in the grass at their feet.
—The man jerks his legs back
and the black lash whips

swiftly—a quaking crevice
on yellow ground. It splits
the dust-mote laden refuge of late

afternoon with a low
winnowing rustle, shoots
like a loosed arrow from the human pair

who—startled—start backward
and freeze to stare.
Its cross-stitched skin glints, slick

with the sun it had lain in, an oiled refraction.
Perhaps it had been basking in wait
for dusk's little animal jolts,

priming its throat. Perhaps
it had made a crushed-grass nest
in the sun's seepage, some golden settlement.

—A gap of pause, in which two moths
list, clumsy and fresh
in ferruginous wings. The humans listen

while the snake hesitates, time hinged
on a break. Then, it slips
into grass blades, yes, but this—it *slips*

up, into the wrangle of branches
of a recently-leaved bush, uses *that*
as a ladder by which to loop

itself to a nearby fir, wires higher
the forked boughs. They hear rasps
of jostled foliage. The slim body of sound

skims bark, twines and writhes,
unfixing leaves, while the pair eye this,
their thoughts lifting

—this being the last thing
from this least thing to expect.
Look! she exclaims, as it reaches one perch

and the bough dips under its weight
(it is a big snake),
almost pours it to dirt. But no: it can bend

for such risk, clamber what's vertical
to a place above their minds
within the fir tree's needled fronds

which cast miniature rungs of shadow
rippling its coat. It lies quietly, mottled
by the softly blown fringe filtering light.

A Cove

What I saw there
traveling with my mother
along that dipping coast

as I peered into small coves,
private, unreachable,
hundreds of feet below

and tossed with lucid water
—a guidebook green-blue ocean
beside a perfectly white-grained shore—

was nothing but the water and the shore
and the black rugged rocks
the ocean rocked against

and the calm, dark, longer reaches
at the horizon above an unseen floor
that verged and slipped, I knew

to desolate fathoms.
It was later I imagined
the fish, stranded in wild water,

what a life might be that lived perpetually moved,
submitted to the crush,
back and forth, of a rocking border,

the fingernail of shore
never an arrival, unless by mistake.
What you won't find in the shallows

of the Pacific's shoreline coves
is the giant clam
whose scalloped shell might be a flute,

an animal which does not move
except to open and close
its shell. But you might discover

hordes of pale crustaceans
gathered and thinned with the tide,
and the grass rockfish

whose scales are the hue of bluegrass,
and the moray eel
whose life began as a silver dart

in some fresh river, and who will,
with its low-slung jaw and giant eyes
kill an octopus,

and the fragile-appearing starfish
who can, with its retractable stomach,
grip and suck

a clam clean of its insides,
and the limpet whose foot strikes the rock,
whose pointed shell looks like a Chinese hat,

and, most telling of all, the small,
circular, coin-like
"sailors-on-the-wind"

so helpless they can go
only where the tide carries. They end
up here, as if cupped in a palm

always tipping, sloshed
to a blue, iridescent phalanx. A bloom
of them may wash up and die

in a gurgle of color, stranded on rocks.
In this spirited flux
it is good to be flexible, like the *postelsia*,

a sturdy plant rooted to the rock.
When the tide blusters and swells, its stalk
bends to touch the ground on one side

and bends to touch the ground on the other,
springing back and forth
in the happenstance current

its fixed, moving life.
When I feel a darkness
I think of the small fish hanging

in their net of mist,
helpless, silent
as wisdom is,

the water's torment
sweeping them from one bare moment
to another, like the wave of a mood.

Unflappable,
occasionally swimming against the current
(but not often), they prove

the case that it may be stronger,
when some force is upon you,
to let yourself

be tugged in the wake of its gesture,
however mindless.
If you wait, and if you move

very slowly, it may catch you in its surge
and hold you as one body holds another body,
and return you to your life.

NOTES

"*Woman Reading to the Sea*": My thanks to Franco Mondini-Ruiz for the inspiration of his painting, titled the same, for the title poem and the title of this book, and for his generosity in providing the use of his painting for the cover.

Epigraph to Part 1: Lines from "Beauty" from *Les Fleurs du Mal* by Charles Baudelaire, translated from the French by Richard Howard. Reprinted by permission of David R. Godine, Publishers Inc.

Epigraph to Part 2 from *Paradise Lost*, Book III, edited by Stephen Orgel and Jonathan Goldberg.

"Hadean Time": That period, approximately 4.5 billion to 3.8 billion years ago, during which the solar system formed and the earth changed from a liquid to a solid state.

"Death and Transfiguration of a Star": Quotations in this poem were taken from Herbert Friedman's, *The Astronomer's Universe*, W. W. Norton and Company: New York, London (1990), p. 19.

First epigraph to Part 3 from *The Aeneid*, Book VI, translated by Robert Fitzgerald.

Second epigraph to Part 3 from *Antiquitez de Rome*, translated by Edmund Spenser.

Epigraph to Part 4 from *A Streetcar Named Desire*, Scene Nine (my addition in brackets).

"Disobedience": I am grateful to Franco Mondini-Ruiz for his insightful assistance with this poem.

"A Cove": Special thanks to my stepfather, Douglas Vaughan, a former marine biologist, who assisted me with some of the details in this poem.